A COMPLETELY NEW EDITION

# Tell me about God

### By MARY ALICE JONES

### Illustrated by DOROTHY GRIDER

RAND McNALLY & COMPANY

## BIBLE REFERENCES *(in order of reference)*

DEUTERONOMY 4:35

GENESIS 1:31

PSALMS 104:1, 14, 15, 27

GENESIS 2:8-9, 15; MARK 12:30

I PETER 5:7

PSALMS 95:1-7; DEUTERONOMY 2:7;
   JAMES 2:14-17

MARK 12:30

JOHN 14:8-11

MARK 5:35-43

MATTHEW 9:9-13

PSALMS 19:1-6

PSALMS 37:3-6

PSALMS 56:3

PSALMS 136:1, 23-26

LUKE 23:34

MATTHEW 6:14

DEUTERONOMY 30:11-14

EPHESIANS 4:32

ISAIAH 43:15

ISAIAH 6:1-8

*Library of Congress Catalog Card Number: 67-15727*

First printing, October, 1967

# Contents

# God Is Real

BOBBY and his daddy had been to the airport to see the big new liner that was beginning service to the nearby city.

"The pilot has a big job," Bobby said as they drove home.

"Yes, he has, Bobby. He worked hard to be ready for it."

"When the airplane is in the air the pilot is almost like God," Bobby went on. "The people have to depend on him."

"People do trust him, son. Maybe we can say a dependable pilot helps us understand the dependability of God."

"I know God is more important than the pilot, Daddy. But the pilot is so real."

"Isn't God real, too, Bobby?"

"We could see the pilot pushing the buttons and hear him giving the signals. God isn't real like that," Bobby said.

Daddy agreed. "No, not real like seeing and touching and hearing. But there are some other very important *reals,* son."

"What are they like, Daddy?"

"Like our knowing right now that Mother and Mary love us.

We can't see them or hear them or touch them. But their love is real to you, isn't it, Bobby?"

Bobby thought a moment. "Yes, it is. I feel it inside me."

Then he laughed. "Something else is real to me, too. I know that Mother will have dinner ready when we get home."

Daddy laughed with him. "And we know it will be good."

Bobby was serious again. "But how does knowing Mother loves me help me to know *God* is real?"

"God is real to us something like the way it is real to you right now that Mother loves you. It is real because over and over again you have felt her love. You have experienced it."

" 'Experienced it,' " Bobby repeated. "That's a big word."

He thought about it. "But I think I know what you mean, Daddy. It's real because I have had it in my own self."

"That is one way of saying it, Bobby. It is something like that when we think about God being real. Over and over again in our own selves we have felt sure the love of God is with us."

"I need to know more about it," Bobby said. "About how God is real."

# Can We Know God?

BOBBY lived next door to John on one side and next door to Susan on the other side. They had been playing catch-the-ball with their dogs. Now they were resting.

"Ginger and Samson and Rover are all good dogs, but they aren't alike," Susan said. "I wonder why there are so many different kinds of dogs."

"Well, I like them to be different," John answered. "It is more interesting." He caught Samson's collar. "I like Samson the way he is."

Just then Bobby's little sister, Mary, and Susan's little brother, Jack, ran over to join them.

Mary threw a ball to Rover. "I like Rover best."

"Dogs!" Jack said.

Bobby laughed. "Jack thinks they are all just dogs."

Susan called Ginger to her. "They are all dogs, but each one is different."

"All people are people, too," Bobby said. "There are more

9

people than dogs, but each one of us is different."

"It makes me wonder," he went on. "There are so many people. How can God know each one of us?"

Susan scratched Ginger's head. "Well, there are lots of dogs the same breed and color as mine, and I would know Ginger anywhere. Wouldn't I, Ginger? So I guess each one of us is special, too. In God's thought, I mean."

Just then Susan's mother called to say it was time for Jack's nap, and Susan took him home. John remembered that he had promised to help his mother clean the basement.

Bobby and Mary went inside and found their mother in the kitchen making a pudding.

Bobby was thinking about all the people. "Mother, there are so many people. How can each one of us be important? To God, I mean."

"I think we don't understand God all at once, dear. But I think we can learn more and more."

"Daddy said God is real like your loving me is real. But I *know* you. Can I know God?"

"No one can know all that God is, Bobby. But I think it is part of the plan of creation that people come to know God. What God is like and what he does are made known to us in many ways."

"Are you sure, Mother? How does God let me know him?"

"Nobody can tell you just how God becomes known to you, dear. You will have to learn for yourself."

"But I want to know right now," Bobby insisted.

His mother smiled. "I know you do, Bobby. Let me tell you one way I felt God was making himself known to me."

"Did he show himself to you, Mother? How did he?"

11

"This morning some of us at a church meeting were wondering how we could be good neighbors to some strangers, two families from the Philippines who have moved into our community. Coming home I saw one of the Filipino mothers walking toward the supermarket. She looked lonesome and tired."

Mother stopped for a moment to test the pudding.

"But, Mother, you were going to tell me how God showed himself to you. Why are you telling me about the Filipino mother?"

"That is how I felt God showed himself to me, dear."

"I don't understand that at all," Bobby said.

"Don't you, son? It seemed to me that God was showing himself to me when I saw someone who needed a friend."

"You mean when you saw the mother who was lonesome and tired you felt that God was there? Because she needed somebody to care about her?"

"That was the way it seemed to me."

"Did you tell her God cared about her?" Mary asked.

"How did you tell her, Mother?" Bobby continued.

Mother took the pudding off the stove. "What do you think the woman needed most right then?" she asked.

"I think she needed a lift to the supermarket," Bobby said.

"And a lift back home with the groceries," Mary added.

Mother nodded. "That is what I decided, too. After we had unloaded her groceries at home I invited her to come to our house tomorrow to meet a few of the neighbors."

Bobby put some spoons in the right place. "Yes, she will like that," he decided. He frowned. "But what if you had hurried by without seeing the tired mother?"

"Often I do get so busy with what I am doing that I forget to see something I should see," Mother agreed. "If I had hurried by this morning I think I would have missed one of the ways

God shows himself to us. The way of showing himself to us through people who need someone to care about them."

Mary looked pleased. "I think that is a nice way."

"But I wish God would show himself to me in a way that is plainer," Bobby said. "So I wouldn't ever miss it."

"People have wished that often, dear. But they have found that when they really want to see what God is showing them they pay more attention, and so come to understand it more and more."

Mother picked up the pudding. Bobby gave a sniff. "That smells good! May I have some?"

"Only a sniff right now! It will be all set when Daddy comes home for dinner."

"Come on, Mary," Bobby called. "Let's go down the street to meet Daddy's car and drive home with him. Then we can have dinner and the pudding."

# God Planned a Good World

BOBBY and John and Susan were in the same room at school.

"I'm glad tomorrow is a holiday," Bobby said as they walked home. "It will be fun to visit Mr. Haven's dairy farm."

Susan gave a skip. "I'm glad your daddy asked us to come."

The next day Bobby's mother and daddy and Mary sat in the front seat of the car and Bobby and John and Susan sat in the back seat and they started out to Mr. Haven's dairy farm.

As they drove along they passed an apple orchard in bloom, and a truck farm where men were gathering beans and lettuce, and a field of grain where men were riding a tractor.

John pointed toward the fields. "There are lots of things to eat growing along this road."

"They are pretty, too," Susan added.

Bobby waved to the men working. "But men have to work to keep things growing," he reminded them. "There isn't a button-pusher who makes apples and cereal and beans pop up out of fields."

Mary sang a little tune, making it up as she sang. "Things are growing, seeds are planted, men are working, the sun is shining, we will have food to eat," she sang.

Bobby and John and Susan laughed as Mary finished. "That was a nice song, Mary," Susan told her.

"But I think you didn't get it right," Bobby said. "You should begin with the sun. Things couldn't grow without it."

John spoke up. "No, but if the seeds weren't planted, the sun could not make them grow. How should Mary's song begin?"

"How do you think it should begin, John? What came first of all?" Mother asked.

"You mean first of all God thought about it? The sun and the earth and the seed and all?"

"Do you think it could just have happened? Without any thought at all?" Daddy responded.

16

Bobby pointed toward the apple orchard they were passing. "It all looks like a plan."

"It looks like a *good* plan," Susan said. "It is pretty and it gives people what they need to eat."

Daddy had come to a crossing, and turned into a side road. Mr. Haven's big white barn was just ahead of them. Soon the dairyman was greeting his visitors.

"There's a baby calf," Mary squealed. Then she looked at Mr. Haven. "He's wobbling. Won't he fall?"

Mr. Haven laughed. "I think not. He's learning fast."

John and Bobby were looking toward the big barn where the cows and milking machines were.

"Can we see the milking machines work?" Bobby asked.

17

"It isn't time for milking yet," the dairyman told them. "But we can see the cows feeding and the barns where we take care of them. Then we can have the picnic my wife has planned for us, and after that it will be time for milking."

They had a fine afternoon in the pasture and the barn and eating a good picnic lunch and then watching the milking machines and the foaming milk.

As the sun was setting they thanked Mr. and Mrs. Haven and drove through the gate.

"I like the Havens and their dairy," John remarked as they turned toward the highway.

"This whole trip has been fun," Susan said. "I liked driving out by the fields and seeing the cows and the milking machines." Then she asked, "Did God plan all of it?"

Bobby answered her. "I think God left the dairy and the milking machines for men to think up. But I think he planned the growing things and the cows and the calves and the milk."

"Just how God planned it all we do not know, Bobby. But we feel sure that purpose and wisdom are back of our world."

"It is a good world," Bobby agreed.

Daddy went on. "I think part of the good purpose is that we should care for our world. Take responsibility for using it wisely to provide for the needs of all people."

Mary was leaning on Mother's shoulder. "I think God wants everybody to have enough food to eat and enough milk to drink and pretty flowers," she said sleepily.

Mother gave her a hug. "I am sure that is part of God's purpose for all his children."

## God Cares About Us

BOBBY and John were puzzled.

"I don't see how he *can* be in our room," Bobby said.

"I don't either," John agreed. "How can he?"

Their teacher had told them that a new boy named Roy was coming to their room the next week. And Roy was blind.

"He can't read our books," Bobby went on. "And he can't know what is on the blackboard, and he can't even see where the doors are. The teacher said he has always been blind."

John was thinking about what might happen. "What will he do on the playground? He might get hurt."

Bobby nodded. "And what will he do in the craft shop?"

That evening Bobby talked with his mother and daddy about the blind boy. "What will he *do* in our room?" he asked.

"I think the boy will be able to get along or the school would not have put him in your room," Mother said. "But I am sure you and John and Susan and all the others in the room will have some extra learning to do."

"What do you mean, Mother? I think Roy will have the learning to do. Why will *we* have extra learning?"

Daddy picked up his glasses and twirled them toward Bobby. "Do you remember the first time you saw me with glasses on?"

Bobby looked surprised. Then he laughed. "Yes, I do, Daddy. It was when I was little. And I got mad at them because you would not take them off when you read to me."

"So you had some learning to do about your daddy's eyes."

Bobby was not sure he understood. "You mean I have to learn about Roy's blind eyes? How can I?"

"You will have to learn what a blind boy can do and what he cannot do, and learn how to get along with him as he is. Just as you had to learn that your daddy could not read to you without glasses, and so you stopped being upset about them."

Bobby remembered. "But why can't Roy see, anyway? I think God would have looked after it."

"There are several causes of blindness, Bobby. I don't know why this boy was born blind. But I know that God cares about him, and wants him to have a good life."

"But, Daddy, you know it is not good for Roy to be blind."

"We do not know all about many of the things that happen in our world. Some things happen that are not good. But we know that whatever happens God cares about us."

"I wouldn't think God cared much about me if I were blind," Bobby insisted.

"Wouldn't you, Bobby? Do you think God forgets you when something happens to you that is not good?"

Bobby thought about it. "You and Mother wouldn't."

"No. Because, you see, we love you. The more you need us, the more we would care about you. That is the way love is."

"Is God like that? Cares about us when we need him most?"

"I am sure of it, son."

Bobby stood up. "But I wonder about that blind boy."

Daddy stood up, too. "So do we, Bobby. It is very hard to understand how a boy can be blind when he needs his eyes so much. But he *is* blind. And he is coming to your school. How can you learn to get along with another boy's blindness?"

Bobby turned to his mother. "Mother, you said the other day that the lonesome woman from the Philippines helped you to understand God's love." He turned back to his daddy. "Is it

like that with the blind boy, Daddy? Can he help me feel God's love? Because he needs love so much?"

"If you feel sure God cares about a blind boy and wants you to care, this will help you to know God better, Bobby."

Daddy sat down on the couch. As Bobby snuggled against him, Daddy went on, "Because Roy is there, your teacher and you and John and Susan and all the other people in your room are going to have a chance to do some special growing in understanding God's care."

"To have a blind boy for a friend will be something new," Bobby said. "Like you said, Mother, I'll have to learn a lot."

## The Bible Helps Us to Know God

JOHN and Susan were at Bobby's house watching TV with him. The new space launching had been perfect and they had heard the explanations from Space Control.

"Was that ever exciting!" John exclaimed. "Someday I'm going up in a spaceship."

"Do you suppose they will ever get it so anybody who wants to can take a trip in space?" Bobby wondered.

"Well, there are lots of places I want to go to on the earth before thinking about going into space," Susan declared.

"That's because you are a girl," John teased.

Before Susan could respond, Bobby asked seriously, "Mother, does the Bible say anything about men traveling in space? One of the boys at school asked if we should do it, because the Bible didn't say anything about it. Maybe God doesn't want us to."

The TV coverage of the space flight was over for a while and Mother turned off the program. "I think the Bible doesn't say anything about what we know today as space travel," she said.

"Then how do we know we should do it?"

Mother asked another question. "Is the Bible just a book of rules, son? Rules that tell us to do this or not to do that?"

Bobby shook his head. "No, that's not right. We decided it is a book about God and what he has done and about men and what they have done."

"Then why didn't it say anything about space travel?" John wanted to know. "We need to know about it."

"Indeed we do, John," Mother agreed. "The Bible tells us what is most important, I think. You remember that in the very first verse of the Bible it says, 'In the beginning God created the heavens and the earth.' "

"Does that include space?" Susan asked.

"I think, Susan, the Bible is saying to us that the whole universe is part of one great purpose."

Bobby went back to the questions of the boy at school.

"But the Bible doesn't say anything about astronauts going into space. Maybe that is God's country, not man's country."

"I think the Bible doesn't say man is shut out that way, Bobby. It tells us that man is to work with God everywhere." Mother took the Bible from the table.

"One of the loveliest parts of the Bible story of creation is this:

And the Lord God planted a garden in Eden,.. . .

And God put (man) in the garden to till it and keep it."

"That's like the men we saw on the way to the dairy. They were helping crops to grow," Susan recalled.

Mother found another place. "When Jesus was talking with his friends about what was most important for men, he said,

'And you shall love the Lord your God with all your heart, and with all your *soul,* and with all your *mind,* and with all your *strength.*'"

John repeated slowly, " 'And all your mind.' Well, if the Bible says we are to love God with all our mind, it means we are to learn. So it must be good to learn about space."

"I think that is the way it is, John. I think the Bible all the way through makes it clear that people are expected to go on learning about creation. All that our minds can learn."

"That tells us something about God, too, doesn't it, Mother?" Bobby said. "It tells us that God isn't just a big boss who makes us do things. We don't understand all about it, but people are to think and plan about it and work in it, too."

"Then maybe the Bible doesn't have to talk about exploring space," John decided. "It tells us God wants us to learn about *everything* he planned."

"Does the Bible tell us everything we need to know about God?" Susan asked. "Can we find all the answers in the Bible about what God is like? And about what he wants us to do?"

28

"The Bible helps us, Susan. We can find out more and more about God as we study the Bible. It tells us how other people came to know God." Mother touched the Bible in her hand. "But this isn't like your dictionary or fact book that you can open at the right place and find exact answers to questions about facts."

"I wish it were like that," John declared. "I wish it told us right out all the answers to all our questions about God and what to do about everything."

"Do you, John? Many people have wished that."

"But if it did, we wouldn't need to love God with our minds, John," Bobby reminded him. "We would be more like your electric train. Just being controlled by somebody pulling a switch."

John sighed. "It's harder when we have to think ourselves. But I wouldn't like it the other way," he agreed. "I guess it's better that the Bible helps us know God. But we have to use our own minds to understand what it says."

## We Worship God

JOHN and Bobby were skating on the frozen pool at the playground. This was the first time they had been able to go around the pool without tumbling.

"Boy, oh boy, was that fun!" Bobby shouted as he came to a smooth stop and caught the handrail.

John gave a gasping laugh. "I'm out of breath, but I feel as if I'd been flying."

"I'm ready to go again," Bobby said. And away they went, twice around this time without a tumble.

The teacher in charge greeted them as they came to a stop. "That was good!" he called. "Soon you can do some figures."

John grinned. "I'd rather learn to go faster."

"You need good control of your body for speed and figures both," the teacher responded. "So let's work on that."

When it was time for the group to leave the pool, Bobby and John slung their skates over their shoulders and hurried home. Bobby told Daddy about the fun he'd had skating.

"I'll have to get back in practice," Daddy said.

"Will you, Daddy? Then you can take John and me to the big rink and we can really get going."

Daddy nodded. "After a little more practice on the small pool, so you have good control of your body."

"The skating teacher said that. What does it mean, Daddy?"

"It means that you think quickly and give signals to your muscles so they do what you want them to do without fumbling."

"Like braking and turning and balancing just right when I am skimming along on the ice?" Bobby asked.

"That's right," Daddy agreed. "It takes practice."

"I think I have good body control," Bobby said. "I can skate and play ball and make things with my hands and swim."

Mother smiled at him. "And carry packages for a neighbor."
Bobby looked at her questioningly. "I was glad you saw that Mrs.
Hunter needed help unloading her groceries from the car."

"That is another important way of body control," Daddy said.
"Deciding to use your body to do something that needs doing."

"It's fun to have a body that can do all sorts of things,"
Bobby declared. "I'm glad I can control my body."

Daddy agreed. "It is part of a good creation." Then he
added, "To use our bodies right is one of the ways we can
worship God."

Bobby seemed surprised. "I thought worshiping God was
when we thank him and listen to the Bible and sing and pray and
ask him to help us. How do we worship God with our bodies?"

"The other day we read about loving God with our minds,"
Mother reminded him. "In that same Bible passage Jesus reminded
his friends also to love God with all their *strength.*"

"I remember that," Bobby admitted, "but I didn't think it was about worshiping. I thought worship was different."

"Many people do think worshiping God is only something for special days or special services in special places like church or around the fireplace at home or saying grace at an outdoor picnic," Daddy responded.

"Isn't that right?" Bobby asked.

"Worship is showing honor and praise to God who is goodness and wisdom and love beyond our knowing."

"But how do we worship God, Daddy, if it isn't by praying and singing?"

"We worship God in church services when we pray together and sing hymns of praise and listen together to the Bible being read. We worship God when we pray here at home. But," Daddy went on, "worshiping does not end when prayers and hymns and Bible reading end, Bobby. If it does, it isn't real worship."

"Tell me more about it. I think I don't understand it very well," Bobby said.

Mother put her arm around Bobby. "Though we cannot understand all of the greatness and love of God, they are always close to us, dear."

"Is that what it means to worship God? To feel his love close to us? But what does my body have to do with it?"

Daddy answered. "It is good to feel the love and goodness of God close to us, son, and sing songs of praise. But to worship God is more. It is also to take part ourselves in the joy and love and goodness in creation. To use our bodies to express joy and to show love and goodness to other people."

"Is that what it means to worship God with our strength?"

"That is an important part of it, Bobby."

Bobby thought about it. "That is a big way to think about worshiping God. With my heart and mind and strength."

# Man's Work

THIS afternoon I am going to see a farmer near the place where the big dam is being built," Bobby's daddy told him one morning at breakfast. "Would you like to go along and take a look at the dam?"

Bobby jumped up. "You know I would, Daddy. Can we ask John and Susan to go, too?"

"That will be fine. Run over before school so they can check with their mothers. I'll pick you up at school."

Daddy gave Mother and Mary a good-bye hug. "We'll be home in time for dinner," he told them as he turned to leave.

The dam was a big project. Bobby and Susan and John watched the giant cranes and the huge concrete-mixing machines noisily grinding away. They watched the workmen moving levers and turning cranks and swinging out in cages from one place to another.

John pointed toward the busy scene. "That is hard work."

"Those men surely know their job," Bobby added.

"I could never handle those machines," Susan declared.

"But somebody *had* to learn how to handle them," Bobby told her. "That dam is needed, isn't it, Daddy?"

"The people in our state need to have the water controlled," Daddy agreed. "The engineers recommended this dam to control the water."

Daddy knew one of the engineers and the man came over to speak to them. They asked questions and learned more about what the various machines were doing. They learned, too, more about how the dam would hold back the water to prevent floods when there were heavy rains, and then let it flow out to provide needed water when there was too little rain.

On the way home they agreed that building a dam was hard work and that the work was important because it let men control the way rain was used.

"I read in a book that some Indian tribes did some dances to control rain," Susan reported. "Does that do any good?"

"Many people through the ages have had ceremonies they performed to try to control weather," Daddy told them. "They thought their ceremonies helped."

"But did they really help?" Bobby asked. "Like dams do?"

John broke in. "My aunt out west where they had a drought last summer wrote us that people were praying for it to rain. Does praying for rain help?"

"Rain dances for rain and praying for rain are very different ways people have of asking God to help them when they need

help," Daddy explained. "I think the people are trying to get in touch with power and love in ways that will help them. Some ways help more than others."

Bobby was thinking. "Is that what the engineers who planned the dam were doing? Bringing needs to God?"

"I am not sure just how those engineers thought about it, son. Maybe they thought of it as working with God. Maybe they thought of it as just a job to control water. But I am sure they could never have been able to build a dam to control water without working with the great purposes of creation."

"Tell us more about it," Susan asked.

"Before the engineers could plan ways to control water they had to have minds that could plan. And their minds had to have laws they could depend on. Natural laws like balance and gravity. The engineers did not make these laws; they discovered them, and had to learn to understand them and to use them."

"But engineers worked," Bobby insisted. "People who do rain dances and pray for rain aren't using their minds and strength

to learn how to control the rainwater themselves. They are asking God to do it all for them."

"It isn't quite like that, I think, Bobby. Rain dances seem strange to us, like magic. Even in praying, I think we need to be careful not to feel we have done all we should do when we talk with God about something that needs doing."

"You mean we should ask God to help us see what we can do about it ourselves?" John asked. "Not expect God to take over and do it all just because we ask him to?"

"I think we are expected to work too, John."

"You and Mother said we must be responsible people," Bobby remembered.

"I guess seeing what needs to be done and getting to work at it is being responsible," John added.

"Those engineers saw what was needed to be done and got

to work at it," Bobby said. "I think working for it is a better way to get water than to pray for the rain to come just at the right time and just in the right amount," he said.

"There are two things to remember, I think, son. One is that keeping ourselves in touch with God's wisdom and love helps us to plan wisely as we could not do by ourselves."

"I see what you mean, Daddy. What is the other thing to remember?"

"The other is that God doesn't do for us what we can do for ourselves."

"You mean there is something we can depend on, but we must be responsible, too?" Bobby asked. "To work and help meet people's needs?"

"I think that is the way it is, Bobby."

# Jesus Shows Us What God Is Like

BOBBY and his daddy were reading in the living room.

"Daddy, what is God really like?" Bobby asked.

Daddy looked up over his magazine. "That is a big question, son. What are you wondering about especially?"

Bobby held up his book. "This book tells about some people who thought the sun is God. We've talked about God, but how can we know what God is *really* like?"

"People have had many thoughts about God, Bobby. No person can ever know all about God."

"But it is important not to make mistakes about God."

Daddy put his magazine aside. "It is not easy for people like us to understand all that God wants to show us. That is why Jesus lived among men."

"Tell me about it, Daddy."

"From the very beginning there was a plan for creation. People were to worship the Creator and love each other and take care of the world. But the years passed and man had a hard

time understanding. God did not *make* men understand. He wanted them to see for themselves. So Jesus lived among men to show them what God is like."

"But Jesus was a man, wasn't he? How could a man show other men what God is like?"

"Yes, Jesus was a man, Bobby. He was born a baby and he grew up as a boy and became a man. His body needed sleep and food as other men's bodies do. He suffered when he was hurt as other men do. But he is different from other men, too."

"How was he different?"

"There is a mystery about it, Bobby. We cannot fully understand it. But we know that as Jesus lived among men they felt closer to God. The people who knew Jesus came to a new experience of God. One that changed everything for them."

42

"What did Jesus show them about God that changed everything, Daddy?"

"He showed them that everybody is important to God. Not just those who were rich and held important positions, but everybody. Little children and beggars and bad people and people from other countries—Jesus cared about them all."

"Yes, Jesus was good to people," Bobby agreed.

"Not just *good* to them, Bobby. When a little girl was very sick and her mother and daddy thought she was dead, Jesus did not just cure her sickness. He really cared about the little girl and the worrying mother and daddy. When he met a man whom all his neighbors disliked and who was lonely, Jesus cared enough about the man to ask him to go with him and become one of his friends and helpers."

"I am glad Jesus was like that," Bobby said.

"Whenever Jesus saw anyone in pain, he really suffered with that one. When he saw anyone who was happy, he rejoiced with that one. When little children came to see him, he took them in his arms and made them glad. Whatever happened to another person mattered to Jesus. He loved them and cared about them."

Bobby thought about it. "Did Jesus show us what God does when we forget about him?"

"Jesus showed us that God is love, son. But Jesus suffered when men refused to accept this love for themselves and to show it to others."

Bobby remembered. "People were mean to Jesus. They hurt him. But when he suffered he forgave them." He thought some more. "Is God really like that, Daddy? Like Jesus showed us?"

"I think we can be sure of it, son."

"Why don't we always remember that?" Bobby asked.

"I wonder about it, too, son. Why do we ever forget it? It is the best news we shall ever hear."

## God Is Very Great

BOBBY'S mother and daddy and Bobby, Susan, and John had gone to the Fourth of July celebration in the big outdoor stadium.

The people stood and sang "America" and gave the salute to the flag. After the mayor told about the celebration, there were some fireworks. Some became pictures that glowed in the darkness, and some became showers of light against the sky.

"The Fourth of July is a fine holiday" Bobby exclaimed. "I'm glad I am an American."

"I'm glad you are an American, too, son," Daddy said. "Ours is a great country. We are grateful for it." He smiled. "Not just on the Fourth of July when we celebrate, but all the time."

As the last burst of light filled the sky, the high school chorus and the city chorus stood together and sang some songs about the country. Then they closed the program with a song which began,

> The heavens are telling the glory of God;
> The wonder of his work displays the firmament.

"I liked that last song," Susan said on the way to the car.

"They sang it the best," John added.

"It was the loudest, too," Bobby said. "They sang it as if they wanted everybody in town to hear it."

Mother laughed. "It would sound more like a compliment, Bobby, if you said the song was 'triumphant' instead of 'loud.'"

"What does 'triumphant' mean, Mother? I wouldn't say that."

"This is a song of praise for the greatness of creation, and so it is full of joy and gladness and glory. 'Triumphant' means some-

thing like that, I think. It is more than just loud, like a football crowd cheering."

Bobby said the word again. "Triumphant! Yes, that sounds right. I think it was good to end the celebration with a triumphant song. After thinking about our country, it was good to think about God."

Daddy unlocked the car and they all got in.

"God is greater even than our country," Susan said.

"The men who founded our country depended on him, Susan. They were sure they could not build a great nation without him."

"Men who explore space today couldn't get along without God, either," John said. "They have to depend on laws they didn't make themselves."

A busload of people leaving the parking lot began singing, "The heavens are telling the glory of God."

"They liked that song, too," Susan remarked. She giggled. "But it isn't as 'triumphant' as the chorus made it."

They all agreed. "They were singing it just for themselves," Mother said. "Maybe they felt 'triumphant' inside."

When their car was away from the lights of the parking lot and they could see the night sky, Bobby pointed. "It looks just like the song said."

"We know more about all the space out there than the people did when they wrote that song," John stated. "We know it's lots greater than they thought."

"I guess God is greater than *anything*," Susan said. "The greatest country or oceans or mountains or *anything* there is."

Bobby added, "God is greater than atomic power, even."

"Or anything men will ever discover," John continued. "Anything man will discover forever and forever." They were all quiet. Then John went on. "It could scare us."

"The greatness of God could be frightening, John," Daddy responded. "But the creation is not just bigness. It is dependable. Men can trust their lives to its laws. Even away beyond the earth where no one has been before."

"God's plans are good, too," Susan added.

"From the very beginning I think God's greatness and his goodness have gone together," Daddy told them. "Though there is much we don't understand, men know they can go on exploring

the universe and learning about it. That it isn't just a big jumble, but that it makes sense."

Bobby stretched. "You know what? I think we should add to the song about the heavens declaring the glory of God. God is greater than he was when they wrote that song."

"Do you think that is the way it is, Bobby?" Mother asked. "Or is it that we know more about the greatness?"

"Will we ever know all about God?" John asked.

"Let's just say it this way, John," Daddy responded. "The more we learn about the universe and about life, the greater God seems to us. It will probably always be this way."

# We Can Trust God

BOBBY and his daddy were out fishing on the river. They each had caught two fine fish, big enough to take home for Mother to cook for supper. They put the fish on the cord they had brought and hung them in the water to keep cool.

Daddy leaned back against a tree trunk and relaxed. "Fishing is a good way to forget your troubles."

Bobby flopped down in the shade. "Yes, it is. I had almost forgotten about Chuck."

"I am sorry about Chuck, son. I know it upset you."

Bobby was remembering again. Chuck had been an important player on the high school football team. Everybody had looked up to him. Then he had cheated. It was in the papers.

"We all trusted him, Daddy. The coach and the other members of the team did, too. He let everybody down."

"Yes, he did. He let himself down, too."

Bobby looked at his daddy. "When we can't trust people we feel all mixed up," he said. "We need to trust people."

"Yes, we do, Bobby. Most people want to be trustworthy."

"Do they, Daddy?"

"We have talked about some of the people in our town we can depend on," Daddy reminded him.

"I thought we could trust Chuck," Bobby countered. "How can I know somebody else won't let me down, too?"

Daddy put his hand on Bobby's shoulder. "You can't know for sure about other people, son. Neither can other people know for sure about us. None of us—you nor I nor any of our neighbors—can be depended on always. None of us is altogether wise and altogether loving."

Bobby looked forlorn. "I don't like it that way."

"But that is the way it is. People are like that. Each of us has a lot of learning to do about how to live."

Daddy smiled at Bobby. "That makes it all the more important to us to know there is something in our lives that can always be depended on."

"What is it, Daddy?"

"We call that something God. God is wisdom and power and love that we can always trust, Bobby, that will never fail us, whatever happens."

Bobby and Daddy were quiet, watching the river. Then Bobby said, "How can I know I can trust God like that?"

"Nobody can tell you exactly how you can come to know it, son. Everybody has to learn it for himself. But people all over the world and year after year who have trusted God have found something real they can always depend on."

"Did they tell us about it?" Bobby wanted to know.

"Many of them did tell us about it. Some people we know today are showing us they trust God."

"Mother said Mrs. Terrill was like that. Even after she couldn't walk. I wondered about it."

"But it is good, isn't it, Bobby? Good that Mrs. Terrill trusts God? The children on our street seem to like to go to see her."

"Yes, we have fun at her house. She likes us and makes us feel good. Is that because she trusts God?"

"Because she depends on God's love, son, even though she can't walk, she can be happy and help other people be happy."

"What does Mrs. Terrill do when she trusts God, Daddy?"

"I think she responds to God's love. Because she is ready to accept it, she finds it is real and it helps her."

"But she did not walk again," Bobby reminded his daddy.

"No, she did not walk again."

"If she trusted God, why didn't he let her walk again? She was good and she trusted God. It doesn't seem fair."

"We do not know, Bobby. Why good people suffer is a hard question. But Mrs. Terrill found strength and courage to do what she could do instead of complaining about what she could not do. She learned to be a good neighbor from a wheelchair."

"Like making us have a good time at her house?"

"That and many other things I have heard about her doing."
Daddy leaned forward from the tree trunk. "Trusting God means
feeling thankful always for love and goodness in our lives. It
means being ready to learn how to be responsible and how to
help other people find love in their lives."

He touched Bobby's hand. "It does not mean we will always
be safe and comfortable, son. But it means we feel sure that
God is working for good with us even when things are not good."

Bobby sat up. "Are you sure we can trust God, Daddy?"

"I am sure God's love and wisdom are with us. Always."

"I am glad we can trust God. It makes things seem better."

A squirrel ran up the tree behind Daddy. Bobby looked at
the scampering squirrel and laughed. "You know what, Daddy?
I'll bet that squirrel is going to get his dinner. Let's get our fish
home so we can have ours."

# God Forgives Us

BOBBY and Daddy were working in their yard. Bobby was clearing out the flower beds, while his daddy was using the big mower. It made so much noise that they could not talk except when Daddy stopped a moment.

At one stop, Bobby called out, "Daddy, let's rest a while."

"We'll take a break after I finish this side," Daddy answered.

Just as he was finishing that side, Mother came out with a pitcher of fruit juice.

Daddy cut off the mower and wiped his face.

"Good! You are just in time." He took the tray Mother had brought and put it on the little table. Mary followed Mother with a plate of cookies.

"We thought our men needed some refreshments," Mother said.

Mother poured the fruit juice and Mary passed the cookies.

"We needed this, didn't we, Daddy?" Bobby said. "We've been working hard."

Mother looked around. "The yard will look nice tomorrow when the high school church group comes to plan the fall work."

Bobby put down his glass. He said slowly, "Mother, is Chuck coming?"

Mother looked troubled. "I hope he is coming, Bobby. I called him and asked him especially to come."

Chuck was a player on the high school football team who had cheated and caused a scandal. He had been popular in high school and in the high school group at Bobby's church. Everybody was upset about it.

"I think he'd be ashamed to come," Bobby said. "After what he did."

Daddy brushed some crumbs off the table. "He is ashamed, Bobby. He knows he did wrong and hurt lots of people. He has apologized."

"But apologizing won't undo what he did," Bobby declared.

"Chuck knows that, son. He knows he can never undo it."

"But how can he come to a meeting where his friends are? I should think he would want to hide."

Mother put the glasses on the tray. "That is what he does want to do, Bobby. That is what I am trying to persuade him *not* to do."

"But why, Mother? Why do you *want* him to come?"

"Because Chuck *needs* to come. He has to go on living, you know."

"But what he did was wrong."

"Yes, dear, it was. He has suffered for it and will probably never forget it. But he has to find a way to start over."

Daddy's face was serious. "It is very important right now that the people who have loved Chuck let him know they are going on loving him. That they aren't going to turn away from him because he did wrong."

"I think I don't understand it," Bobby said.

"There is something we can understand, son. We can understand that all of us sometimes do what we know is wrong."

"Yes, we do, Daddy, but not *big* wrongs like cheating on the team and hurting the school and everything," Bobby insisted.

"We can't measure wrongs quite that way."

Bobby thought about it. "Is that what you mean by wanting Chuck to come to the meeting, Mother? So you can show him you aren't turning away from him?"

"I think, dear, I want to show him that we don't feel we are altogether good and he is altogether bad. We know what Chuck did was bad. We also know we all fail to be what we were created to be. We all have to depend on God's forgiveness."

"Will God forgive Chuck?" Bobby asked.

Daddy waited a minute. "What do you think about it, son?

Bobby remembered. "We decided Jesus showed us what God is really like." He remembered some more. "Jesus forgave people who were mean to him. When they hurt him. When they did things worse than Chuck did."

"Jesus showed us God's love. It doesn't stop when we turn against him. What we have done is not undone. But the forgiving love of God helps us to make our lives over."

Bobby looked at his daddy and mother. "I guess you are right, Mother, about wanting Chuck to come. Because God loves him, you know God wants you to help Chuck start over."

Daddy stood up. "I am sure of it, Bobby." He moved toward the lawn mower. "And now you and I must get the lawn ready for Mother's group tomorrow."

# When We Listen to God

IT WAS a dark, rainy day. Bobby and John had planned to watch the high school football team practice. They had just decided it was too cold and rainy to have any fun out-of-doors. So Bobby was feeling gloomy.

"I wish it would rain on school days," he said crossly. "Why does it have to rain on days we could go places?"

His mother was running the vacuum cleaner, so she did not answer, and Bobby felt even crosser. He wandered about the house wondering what he could do.

The vacuum cleaner stopped and Mother called, "Bobby, will you help dust?"

Bobby thought dusting was not anything interesting to do; so he was frowning when he picked up the dustcloth.

"I am sorry you are disappointed about watching football," his mother said. She smiled at him. "But, you know, the world has not fallen apart."

Bobby moved a vase carefully as he dusted a table. "But

everything seems so dull today, Mother." He looked at the rain pouring on the windows. "I want something to *do* that's fun."

"When we finish cleaning up, we can ask John and Susan to come over and pop corn in the basement," Mother suggested. "Maybe there is something you would like to have me read."

Bobby looked a little more cheerful. "That is as good as we can do on a day like this," he said. "I have a new book."

The corn popping and the story reading turned into a gay little party, and the dreary afternoon proved to be pleasant.

After Susan and John had gone home, Bobby suddenly asked, "What is my conscience, Mother?"

"Conscience isn't easy to describe, Bobby. We learn that some ways of living and treating people are good and some ways are bad. We say our conscience tells us."

"I thought God told us," Bobby said. "Is conscience just another word for God?"

Mother put away the corn popper. "I think God is much more than our conscience, dear. Responding to God's love and wisdom is the best way, I think, for us to grow in our own understanding and love. In this way we can have a conscience we can depend on."

"I was wondering about consciences getting mixed up." Bobby said. "When we were watching the high school football players the other day, one of them said, 'My conscience would hurt me if I did that.' Another one said, 'Well, my conscience would say I was doing right.' "

"It sometimes comes about just that way, Bobby. People grow up with different thoughts about what is right and what is wrong, and so they have consciences that differ."

"Then how does God tell us?"

"We aren't likely always to be sure, son. We do not always respond to God's love and wisdom, even when we try."

"But if God wants to help us, why can't we?"

"We have to learn to listen to God, Bobby. Sometimes we are too noisy shouting our own ideas to listen. Sometimes we do not want to listen. We want to do what we want to do. Sometimes we are feeling sorry for ourselves about something we can't do."

Bobby grinned. "That is the way I was feeling this morning." He looked at his mother. "But I did hear what you said. How can I hear when God wants to help me decide what to do?"

"One way of listening to God is to use our mind to think and remember, so our conscience can grow."

"You mean to remember what we have already learned about what is a good way to do?"

"I think remembering is a part of listening, Bobby."

"Tell me some more about it."

"In church last Sunday the minister read a passage from the Bible that says something about it, I think. It says:

It is not too hard for you, neither is it far off. It is not in heaven, that you should say, 'Who will go up to heaven and bring it to us, that we may hear and do it?' Neither is it beyond the sea, that you should say, 'Who will go over the sea for us, and bring it to us, that we may hear and do it?' But the word is very near to you; it is in your mouth and in your heart, so that you can do it."

Bobby thought about it. "That sounds as if it is easy. But I don't think it is easy to listen to God."

"It is not always easy to listen, Bobby. But wanting to hear helps us to listen with our own minds and hearts."

"But how do I hear what God says to me, Mother?"

"Sometimes it is very simple, like an idea that comes to you about something that will make someone happy."

"Did God give you the idea of the popcorn and reading?"

Mother laughed. "Well, it was a good idea, wasn't it, son? We had a pleasant afternoon instead of a cross one." They left the basement. "But I did not hear any voice telling me to suggest popping corn."

Bobby thought some more. "No, I think God's plan for helping people was already in your mind. Like the Bible said."

"Not always, Bobby. Often I forget."

Bobby went on with his own thoughts. "Because you had listened to God lots of times you knew how to think up good ideas on a rainy day instead of scolding us for being cross."

"It isn't like magic, Bobby. We make mistakes. We have to learn to listen by trying to listen."

"I want to listen," Bobby said. "How do I begin?"

"I think we are reminded by everyday things. Like obeying the traffic light. Or helping Susan to look after Jack. Or watering Mrs. Terrill's flowers while she is sick."

"That is what you mean by growing a conscience, isn't it? Listening to God so there is something inside us to remind us about ordinary things?"

"We learn in many ways as we live, Bobby. I think there are also special helps for us."

"That's what I want to know. What are they?"

"Are you sure you don't know some of them, Bobby?"

Bobby started to shake his head. Then he stopped and looked at his mother. "You mean like the Bible and Jesus? That they are special ways of helping us to listen?"

"I think they are, dear. I think God's love and wisdom are near to each one of us, helping us to understand. But we need to check up on our own understanding."

"Do the Bible and Jesus help us to check up?" Bobby asked. "To find our mistakes? And get better ideas?"

"Many people find that this is the way it is, Bobby."

## "Holy, Holy, Holy"

BOBBY and John and Susan had been to a science fair. They had seen new types of engines and new hybrid flowers and new ways of freezing foods and new computers.

Bobby's daddy picked them up in his car.

"Scientists can do almost anything," John announced.

Bobby agreed. "I don't see how they can think up all those things we saw."

"Well, I am glad they can," Susan said. "What they have learned makes things nicer for us. Like frozen foods."

Bobby turned to his daddy. "But even scientists don't know everything, do they, Daddy?"

"The wisest scientists would be the first to tell you how much there is yet of mystery in the universe."

"Mystery? What is mystery?" Bobby wanted to know.

Daddy waited for the light to change. "After the studying and experimenting and exploring men do," he explained, "there is always something beyond their knowing."

"But why do scientists stop exploring?" John asked.

"They do not stop trying, John. But they come to the place where their questions cannot be answered by science."

"Why can't all questions be answered by science, Daddy?"

"That is what we mean by mystery, Bobby."

John was puzzled. "What questions can't science answer?"

"Some important questions, John. Like how did the laws scientists depend on come to be? Why people can plan and love and be happy. Why good people suffer."

"Then what do people do about these questions?" Bobby wanted to know. "They need to have some answers."

"Yes, son, people need some answers science cannot give. We call these answers of faith."

"What is an answer of faith?" John asked. "Does it mean the scientists are wrong?"

"Not wrong, John. But scientists are men. Beyond all men can learn is the greatness, power, and love we call God."

"Is mystery to us not mystery to God?" Susan asked.

"Let me get it straight, Daddy," Bobby persisted. "Is it that there *are* answers but we can't know them?"

John was frowning. "I thought we said God wants us to understand. Why does he keep secrets from us?"

Daddy waited a moment. "I think we have minds so we can understand our world. To learn all we can about it. Yet always men have found a limit to what they can understand."

"I think that means there is greatness and wisdom more than man can understand," Susan said.

"More than wisdom and greatness, Susan. There is something called holiness, too. We say God is beyond our knowing."

"That is a big idea," John said. "It is too big for me."

"It is too big for any of us, John. Sometimes we use poetry and hymns to help us. Like the words of this hymn:

> Holy, Holy, Holy, Lord God Almighty:
> All thy works shall praise thy name
> In earth and sky and sea;
> Holy, Holy, Holy, there is none beside thee,
> Perfect in power, in love and purity."

They were all quiet. Bobby looked at Daddy. "We need a God like that for space and the universe and all the nations. But when I think of it, I feel I can't be important."

"The holiness of God does make us feel small, son. But here we find another mystery," Daddy told them, "the greatest mystery of all. The holiness and greatness beyond our knowing is also near to each of us, concerned about us. We can trust God."

"You mean trust him about the things we can't understand? That the scientists can't answer?"

"That is the way it is, I think. Beyond all that the wisest men can learn is always the greatness and holiness of God. And he cares about each of us."